BEHIND

THE

LEGEND

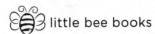 little bee books

New York, NY
Copyright © 2017 by Little Bee Books
All rights reserved, including the right of reproduction in whole or in part in any form.
Manufactured in China RRD 0621

Library of Congress Cataloging-in-Publication Data
Names: Peabody, Erin, author. | Rivas, Victor, illustrator.
Title: The Loch Ness monster / by Erin Peabody; illustrated by Victor Rivas.
Description: First edition. | New York, New York: Little Bee Books, [2017]
Series: Behind the legend; #1 | Audience: Ages 8–10. | Audience: Grades 4–6.
Identifiers: LCCN 2016024308 | Subjects: LCSH: Loch Ness monster—Juvenile literature.
Monsters—Scotland—Juvenile literature. | Classification: LCC QL89.2.L6 P43 2017
DDC 001.944—dc23 | LC record available at https://lccn.loc.gov/2016024308

ISBN: 978-1-4998-0423-2 (pbk)
First Edition 10 9 8 7 6 5 4 3
ISBN: 978-1-4998-0424-9 (hc)
First Edition 10 9 8 7 6 5 4 3 2 1

For information about special discounts on bulk purchases,
please contact Little Bee Books at sales@littlebeebooks.com.

littlebeebooks.com

BEHIND THE LEGEND

THE
LOCH NESS
MONSTER

by Erin Peabody

illustrated by Victor Rivas

little bee books

CONTENTS

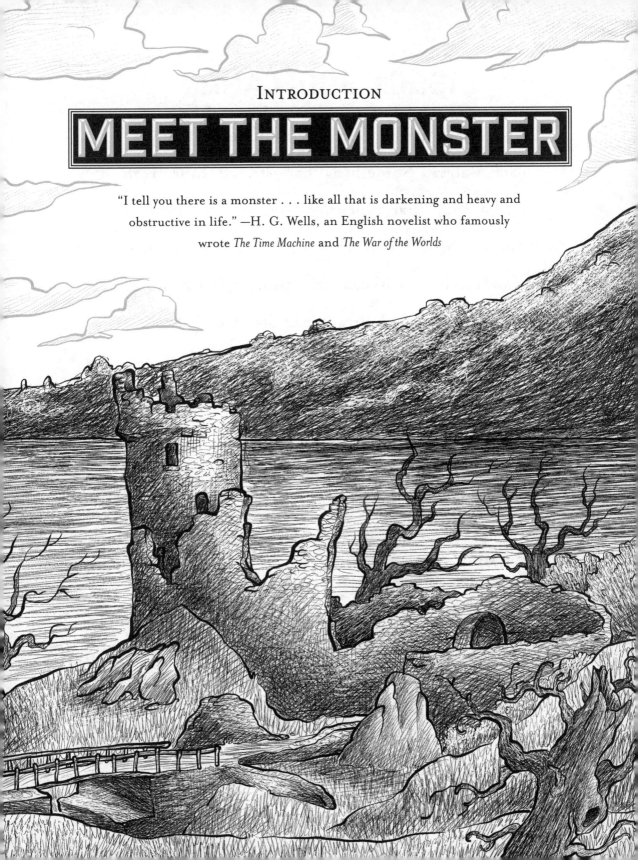

INTRODUCTION
MEET THE MONSTER

"I tell you there is a monster . . . like all that is darkening and heavy and obstructive in life." —H. G. Wells, an English novelist who famously wrote *The Time Machine* and *The War of the Worlds*

1960s, SCOTLAND

It was dawn as the man gazed out across the ink-black waters. Something had stirred him from bed at four that morning. Was it intuition? A premonition? Whatever it was, he felt compelled to start driving without even pausing for a cup of hot coffee or splash of water to the face.

The man, F. W. Holiday, an English journalist and wildlife researcher, was cruising along the shoreline of one of the deepest, darkest lakes in the world: Scotland's Loch Ness (a lake that is twenty-two miles long and about seven-hundred-fifty-feet deep). That's when Holiday first spied it, something splashing violently in the water.

The sight made him gasp "like a stranded codfish," he later wrote in a book about his Loch Ness adventures. Stunned, Holiday grabbed his binoculars and zeroed in on a bizarre "black and glistening" object in the lake. It rose up about three feet then plunged back beneath the dark water, creating such large rocking waves that it reminded him of a "diving hippopotamus." Holiday estimated its size to be about forty-five-feet long.

Of course, there are no hippos in the cool, damp glens and lochs (lakes) of Scotland, the northern country that sits atop England and is mostly surrounded by sea.

No, Holiday was certain of what he'd just seen. It was the great Loch Ness Monster, a spectacular aquatic beast that would consume his thoughts for the rest of his life.

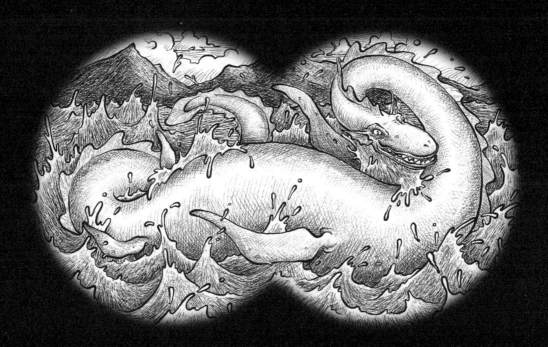

CHAPTER ONE

OF LEGENDS AND LORE

"What grim aspects are these, these ugly-headed monsters? Mercy guard me!"
—John Milton, an English poet

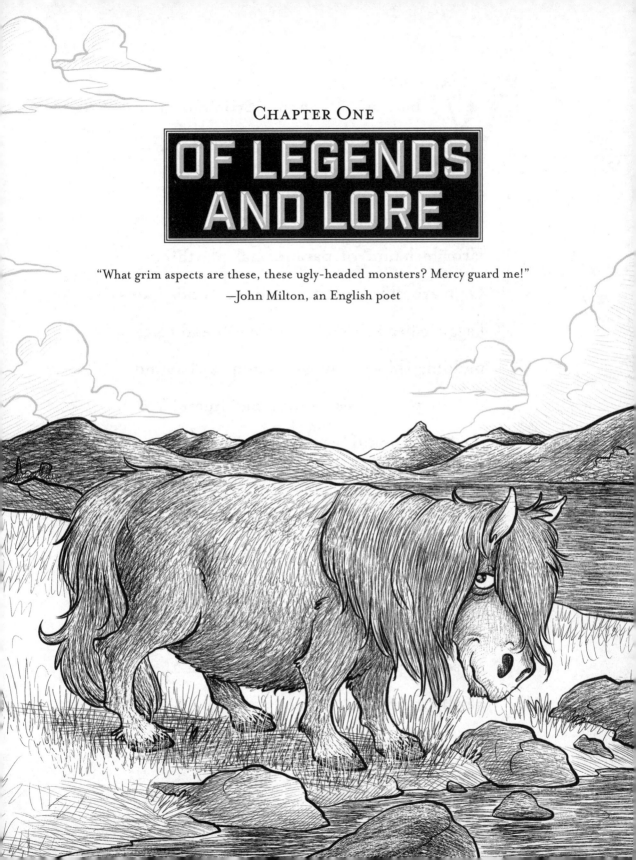

What is it about Scotland that inspires so many terrible tales? Is it the chronic damp air? The ancient crumbling castles that cling to cliffs, a favorite haunt of paranormal playthings? Or maybe the unusual cuisine? Foods like haggis (sheep stomach, anyone?) and black pudding (blood sausage, mmm . . .) sound like the perfect recipe for a nightmare! Yes, the Scots should be as well known for their hair-raising beasties as they are for their verdant golf courses, gaudy print plaids, and bagpipe bands.

Take "kelpies," for instance. They sound charming, like a whimsical line of sea-inspired toys to collect. But that's hardly the case. A kelpie, a creature feared by generations of Scots, is basically a horror movie's version of My Little Pony.

Gentle looking, the small horses were said to graze near the water's edge, waiting for children to approach them or even climb atop their backs.

But once the innocent babes mounted these predatory ponies, their fates were sealed. Instantly, the children would become stuck to the animals, which would then race into the water, not stopping until they'd dragged their poor victims to the

bottom to drown. And then the kelpies would eat them!

But wait, there is a *slightly* uplifting version. In it, the child who reaches out to touch the beast escapes, but only after cutting off his own finger!

MORE SCARY SCOTS

You've heard of killer whales. Well in Scotland, ancient rumors have long swirled about killer seals. Known as "selkies," these sinister shape-shifting creatures were said to morph from seal to human and back to seal again. Like kelpies, selkies were also deceitful, often luring their victims into love affairs that would tragically end.

Other beasts believed to haunt Scotland's dark, frigid waters include the particularly gruesome "buarach-bhaoi," also known as the wizard shackle. This nine-eyed eel (as if eight eyes aren't scary enough!) would lurk in shallow waters near the shore waiting for its next victim—typically a horse or human—to pass by. Then it would lunge, twisting itself around its victim's ankles and dragging its prey underwater to drown. Finally—gag alert!—the leechlike slitherer would suck its victim's blood, which would then squirt from the eel's multiple eye sockets.

Another dreaded creature whose name alone will send shivers down your spine is . . . wait for it . . . the dreaded "BOOBRIE!" Lest you chuckle too hard, you should know that a boobrie is a giant carnivorous bird that ambushes its victims near the shores of lakes and bays. Possessing a

large hook-shaped beak for tearing into meat, it would hide in the reeds, waiting for small hapless creatures—lambs, calves, and children—to stumble into its lair.

Given such ghastly stories, it's a wonder that wee little Scots ever got to sleep at night. But, kidding aside, could there be any truth to these horrific creatures?

CRYPTIDS: UNCONFIRMED CREEPIES

The Loch Ness Monster, or "Nessie" as it's been nicknamed, sure seems to fit in with Scotland's crew of motley characters. But Nessie is a modern-day enigma or mystery—a "cryptid," to be exact. Cryptids are mysterious creatures that scientists have not yet documented, but some folks would swear that they've seen.

Other famous cryptids include Bigfoot or Sasquatch, the hairy hiker of America's Pacific Northwest. Its snowy mountain equivalent is the Yeti, aka the Abominable Snowman. There's also "Mokele Mbembe," the lone, lost dinosaur of Africa's Congo Basin.

Cryptids sound far out. That's typical. They're often large, possess mismatched body parts (think mermaids), and can be hairy, slimy, or smelly.

These bizarre monstrosities all sound pretty ridiculous. So why entertain their possibility at all?

GOTCHA!

There are cases, as cryptid believers are apt to point out, where one-time mystery animals have been proven to exist. Then, officially welcomed by the scientific community, these formerly shunned weirdos are granted beautiful-sounding Latin names and assigned places on the giant family tree of living things.

One of the best examples of a now confirmed cryptid is the world's largest lizard, the Komodo dragon (which can weigh more than three hundred pounds!). But in the mid-1800s, when rumors of the giant lizard starting wafting from the Southeast Asian island country of Indonesia, most Western scientists scoffed at the scaly sensation. A ten-foot-long lizard known to devour both men and water buffalo?! The large lizard believers, the experts assumed, must be having visions of dinosaurs, creatures that had died out eons before.

But then, when World War I ended and scientific exploration around the globe resumed, proof of a mega monitor lizard could not be denied. Explorers delivered the gold standard of evidence when it comes to cryptids—the sword in the side of disbelief: REAL LIVE specimens! They presented scientists with two live dragons, plus about a dozen others that were dried and preserved. So, in 1912, the tongue-flicking Komodo dragon, with jaws full of deadly saliva, was finally ushered into the shimmering halls of science. (Greetings, Dragon Breath!)

Another example is the okapi, a relative of the giraffe, who also suffered a similar shunning. This striking jungle ungulate (that's an animal with hooves) had been known for centuries by the tribal peoples of central Africa, where it still lives today. The Egyptians, who were also enamored by the okapi and its strangely striped legs, scrawled its likeness onto stone. But it wasn't until 1901, when hides and a skull belonging to the animal were thrust before experts, that European scientists finally accepted what they had mockingly dubbed the "African unicorn." Even today, little is known about this secretive leaf-eater whose brilliant stripes help keep it hidden among the scattered shadows of the jungle.

As you can see, both Mother Nature and the human imagination can be awfully (actually, terrifyingly!) creative. Certainly there are amazing creatures all around us, including some whose existence has startled even the stuffiest scientists. But we cannot confuse proven natural wonders with made-up myths and legends.

That's where kelpies and selkies and boobries (oh my!) come in. This may come as a relief, or a bummer, but these wicked wackos are indeed the stuff of myths and legends. Problems happen when monster hunters get so caught up in the chase that

they confuse ancient legends with modern-day sightings or other kinds of evidence.

For instance, some Nessie believers argue that ancient stories about scary serpents in Loch Ness provide historical proof that Nessie indeed exists. However, as devilishly delicious as these stories are, they were totally spun in fun—likely told 'round crackling fires to pass time during the long Scottish winters.

So what about stories or accounts that relate specifically to the modern marvel that is Nessie? There are plenty. Over the past eighty years, thousands of eyewitness accounts describing some kind of large writhing lake creature have streamed in. One sighting in particular took the world by storm, kicking off a tsunami of sightings. It came from a man who was so convinced of the monster that he said he'd even take an oath, swearing on his life that it exists.

A HIDDEN PLANET AND A GAS

Gotta love etymology. The study of words' origins can explain so much. Take the root for cryptid, which is "crypt." It comes from the Greek word *kryptos*, and means "hidden." Know of any other "crypt" words?

There's "Krypton," the home planet of Superman and Supergirl. According to the story, this imaginary planet, created by two comic artists in the 1930s, was utterly destroyed. No life was thought to come from it, until the once-hidden Superman was rocketed to Earth.

You may know the other Krypton from science class. This element, with the official abbreviation Kr and the atomic number 36, is aptly named. It's a colorless, odorless, tasteless gas which has great uses in photography and fluorescent lighting.

CHAPTER TWO

"WE SAW THE MONSTER!"

"Many a man has been hanged on less evidence than there is for the Loch Ness Monster." —G. K. Chesterton, an English writer and philosopher

The man so convinced that he'd seen the Loch Ness Monster was George Spicer. This Londoner's report to a local paper set off a frenzied hunt for the lake creature and spawned hundreds, eventually thousands, of jaw-dropping anecdotes and sightings.

In July 1933, Spicer and his wife were cruising along a freshly paved road adjacent Loch Ness when suddenly Mrs. Spicer cried, "What on earth is that?!"

Lumbering across the road in front of them was "the most extraordinary form of an animal," George Spicer later recalled. "It was horrible, an abomination."

In his account to the paper's editor, Spicer painted a picture of Nessie that is now well known in popular media. The creature was the color of a "dirty elephant," he said, and looked prehistoric—like a long-necked dinosaur. It measured about thirty feet long and appeared to be dragging a lamb or other small animal.

SIGHTINGS POUR IN

Spicer's report set off a firestorm. Locals, tourists, and other curiosity seekers descended upon Scotland's Loch Ness, looking hard for the famous water-dwelling beast. Amazingly, many were supposedly successful.

Observers were struck by Nessie's movements. In some reports the mighty creature thrashed through the water, creating a violent ruckus. The word "violent" or "violently" is found repeatedly across the history of Loch Ness Monster accounts.

But in others, the bulbous beast with a periscope-like neck propels itself quietly and stealthily through water. As one witness recalled, it cut seamlessly through the water "like a yacht."

Regardless of the finer details—which range widely from one account to another—all witnesses share in the absolute astonishment of it all. Consider these statements made by modern-day eyewitnesses who have claimed to have laid eyes on Nessie:

EVEN CYNICS KEEP AN OPEN MIND

An assortment of Nessie spotters across the decades—including doctors, lawyers, accountants, and university students—are confident of what they've seen. Even hardened fishermen who have spent decades on the water and have witnessed a host of curious sights cannot completely dismiss the possibility that some kind of Loch Ness creature exists.

When a group of local fishermen was asked in the 1960s if they had ever seen an odd creature out on Loch Ness, one fisherman responded, "Ye see some weird things out there." His fellow angler responded similarly as he gazed out on the deep lake: "I widdna stay out there after dark for all the tea in China."

Could all these witnesses be wrong though? Could there be a strand of truth in what they've claimed to have seen? Or like the straight-talking Scots, do you say "Yer bum's oot the windae"? (Translation: You're talking nonsense!)

A MONSTROUS PRONUNCIATION

In Scotland, a "loch" is simply a lake, or an inlet of the ocean. That part is easy.

What's not simple, however, is saying the word. In Gaelic countries, such as Scotland and Ireland, the "ch" combination is not pronounced like a hard "k" or "ck" sound, as in duck or truck. Nor is it pronounced like the German "ch" sound, as in Sebastian Bach.

The Scottish "ch" is more throaty and harsh sounding. Imagine that you have a small piece of popcorn kernel shell caught in the back of your throat, and that you're trying to dislodge it. *That* is the sound. And if you're having trouble, you can find pronunciation guides on the Internet.

Just don't practice too much. You might end up with a sore throat!

CHAPTER THREE

HOAXES AND HUCKSTERS IN THE LAND O' HAGGIS

"Oh, what a tangled web we weave, when first we practice to deceive!"
—Sir Walter Scott, a Scottish novelist

When it comes to fantastic creatures such as Nessie, there are cases of mistaken identity. There are also cases of faked, or made-up, identity. Unfortunately, human nature dictates that some individuals won't be satisfied with simply musing or

marveling about spectacular creatures. Instead, they feel the need to exploit them—out of greed, a desire for fame, or in anger. You might say that these tricksters, intent on scaring people or making money, are the real monsters in the history of cryptids.

BRAVADO AND THE BEAST

In December 1933, the same year George Spicer's alleged sighting was causing a stir, the United Kingdom's *Daily Mail* decided to launch an official investigation into Scotland's supposed slithery beast. The paper hired actor and well-known big-game hunter Marmaduke "Duke" Wetherell in the hopes of his landing an extraordinary discovery.

The showy Englishman, a silent film actor and director turned safari leader, had already tromped across portions of Africa. Now he was poised to flush out his next beastly target, with an entourage of reporters and a photographer to boot.

What spectacular luck the party enjoyed. According to Wetherell it took only forty-eight hours of searching the shores of Loch Ness before the hunter discovered large tracks, multiple ones, presumably made by the mysterious brute!

"You may imagine my great surprise," he later exulted during a television interview, "when on a small patch of loose earth, I found fresh spoor, or footprints, about nine inches wide, of a four-toed animal." Wetherell made it sound easy. One of the tracks, he boasted, was "only a few hours old . . . and where I expected to find it."

The news electrified Scotland and much of the rest of the world. Tourists filled the hotels and jammed the local roads in Loch Ness, a region now consumed with monster mania.

"HIPPO"CRATIC OATH

Given the hoopla surrounding Nessie, it was easy to forget that one important piece of business remained: scientific scrutiny of the prints. To that end, plaster molds of the so-called monster tracks were made and sent to experts at London's distinguished Natural History Museum.

It was just a matter of waiting for the people of Loch Ness and for observers across the globe. Scientific confirmation was only a formality, right? Or so thought editors at the *Daily Mail*, the paper that had sponsored Wetherell's trip. The paper, too antsy to hold its juicy story any longer, decided to forge ahead with this front page stunner on December 21, 1933:

Daily Mail

MDCLVII

NO MORE SURRENDERS

MONSTER OF LOCH NESS IS NOT LEGEND BUT A FACT!!

A SCIENTIST investigating the existence of the Loch Ness monster refused to dismiss the popular legend yesterday, in spite of the most famous picture of the supposed creature being exposed as a hoax.

Adrian Shine, leader of the Loch Ness and Morar Project set up to discover whether a mysterious being inhabits the deep waters southwest of Inverness, even welcomed the revelation that the photograph which appeared in the *Daily Mail* in April 1934 was a fraud.

According to new claims, the picture was concocted using a toy submarine fitted with the head and neck of a sea serpent made from plastic wood. It was taken by Colonel Robert Wilson, a Harley Street gynaecologist, who claimed to have seen "some-

game hunter, who had been hired by the *Daily Mail* to track down the monster. The other members of the group were Wetherell's son Ian, his stepson Christian Spurling, and Maurice Chambers, an insurance broker, all of whom are now dead.

that he was convinced that the report of the hoax was valid. Much of the research was carried out by one of his own staff, Alastair Boyd. "It was always a very controversial photograph," he said. When the negative was inspected, the "monster" was found to be very small.

Wetherell is said to have been motivated by revenge after his "discovery" of foot-

But Mr Shine added: "Eye witness acounts still suggest

Wetherell is said to have been motivated by revenge

Unfortunately, this tabloid-like move didn't bode well for the *Daily Mail,* which soon became the butt of many jokes. That's because, in relatively short order, museum scientists came out with their bruising announcement: Wetherell's whopping nine-inch-wide tracks didn't belong to any monster. They were made using the dried, shriveled foot of a hippopotamus! The prop used to make the prints was apparently a safari

souvenir—a silver ashtray mounted to a hippo foot—later found in the Wetherell family's possession!

Most researchers are now convinced that the one-time film director—"a vain attention seeker" as one Loch Ness investigator put it—orchestrated the great hoax. Which explains why soon after the hippo revelation, Wetherell, presumably humiliated, slunk out of sight. Before slipping away to London, though, he denied having any involvement in the big prank.

But like the phantom lake beast itself, the slippery showman seemed bound to resurface again.

NESSIE'S FAMOUS MUG SHOT

Despite the fallout from the hippo hoax, the search for Nessie remained strong. Accounts from eyewitnesses continued to pour in. Only now, people insisted on remaining anonymous for fear of being publicly ridiculed. For its part, the *Daily Mail* suffered major embarrassment, as local papers took turns chuckling at its expense.

But it seemed nothing could tamp down monster madness, especially when a few months later, the most tantalizing piece of evidence was delivered: an actual photo of a long-necked dinosaur-like creature gliding through the loch's rippling waters!

Like George Spicer's description, the creature in the photo looked like a long-lost plesiosaur—a large swimming reptile with powerful flippers that would have surged through Earth's waters about sixty-six million years ago.

The eerie black-and-white photo caused an immediate buzz. And who couldn't resist snatching up another tempting morsel of Nessie news? Why the incorrigible *Daily Mail*, of course! Apparently the paper thought this bulletproof photo would deliver much-needed vindication after the footprint scandal. They saw it as proof that they had been right about Nessie from the start.

What made the photo seem so credible was the respectability of the gentleman who'd snapped it. He was war veteran and London physician Robert K. Wilson. According to Wilson's account, he was driving along Loch Ness when he suddenly spotted an unusual commotion in

the water. Fortunately, the doctor had a camera with him, a rather hi-tech one for the 1930s, and managed to capture what he later described as, "the head of some strange animal rising out of the water." The picture, known as *The Surgeon's Photograph*, quickly became the most famous image of Nessie of all time.

Right away, though, the critics offered up alternative explanations. They argued that the object was mistakenly identified and was really a floating bird, or an otter, or the dorsal fin of a whale. Others clung to the idea—and a few still fiercely do—that the photo is genuine.

A CONFESSION, DECADES LATER

We now know for certain that the picture does not trace back to any monster, but to a familiar prankster rearing his head. Apparently feeling jilted over his earlier ridiculed monster tracks, big-game hunter Marmaduke Wetherell re-emerged to plot another hoax, this one in retaliation.

The general public, however, remained hoodwinked for decades. It wasn't until 1975, in a small article in London's *The Sunday Telegraph,* that Wetherell's son, Ian Wetherell, admitted that the whole thing was a joke. Apparently Marmaduke Wetherell was so angered over the earlier episode with the tracks that he plotted revenge—even remarking to his son: "All right, we'll give them their monster."

And that they did, after first stopping by Woolworth's for a toy submarine that cost two shillings, six pence. Onto this the father and son duo attached a model of a dinosaur head that they made from wood and plastic.

Then they set their creation adrift on the water, where Wilson—the willing photographer—agreed to snap the picture and play along with one of the biggest hoaxes of that era.

Motive is hard to prove, especially when all the principal players are no longer living.

But researchers who have extensively studied Marmaduke Wetherell's case believe that Wilson—who knew the flamboyant actor/hunter through a common acquaintance—went along with the trick simply to be a good sport. Little did the respected London doctor know that the silly prank would snowball into one of history's biggest hoaxes.

Even more evidence for the hoax emerged in 1990, when another relative of Marmaduke Wetherell's, this time his stepson, admitted that the picture was not at all real. "It's a load of codswallop," he remarked flatly, "and always has been."

Hoaxes and pranks are an important part of Nessie's history. Frustratingly, they've clouded the legitimate hunt for any kind of cryptic Loch Ness creature through their deception and their capacity to stoke monster mania.

Whether sleuthing the Loch Ness Monster, Bigfoot, or the Yeti, a good cryptid hunter must tread carefully through these thickets of lies and deception.

ONE BIG PRANK

People love a good prank. History offers up many examples of the elaborate lengths folks will go to fool their fellow humans. One case, which also involved an alleged sea monster, took place in 1904 on Lake George in upstate New York.

The trickster, esteemed New York City artist Harry Watrous, engaged in the most elaborate hoax. He created a large carved wooden monster,

which, thanks to a system of pulleys he designed, appeared to rise up from the lake. And the creative artist didn't scrimp on details, adorning the "monster" with large, green glass eyes, blue ears, and a head covered with black and yellow stripes! Thirty years later, the much-aged prankster finally admitted to orchestrating the fraud. And given the current hype at the time focused on the Loch Ness Monster, that wasn't the only hoax the old man had an opinion on. Scotland's Nessie, as he saw it, was nothing more than a big hoax, too.

Guess it takes one to know one.

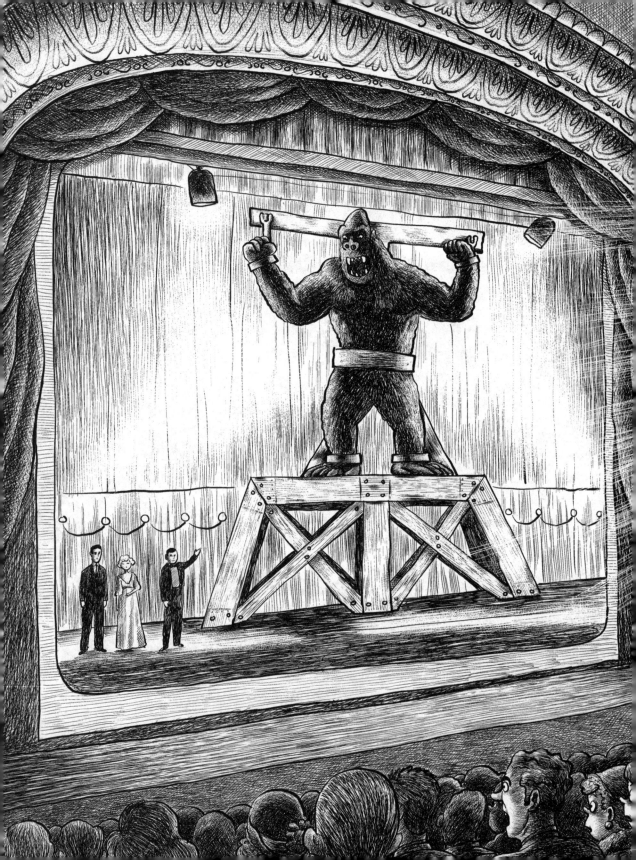

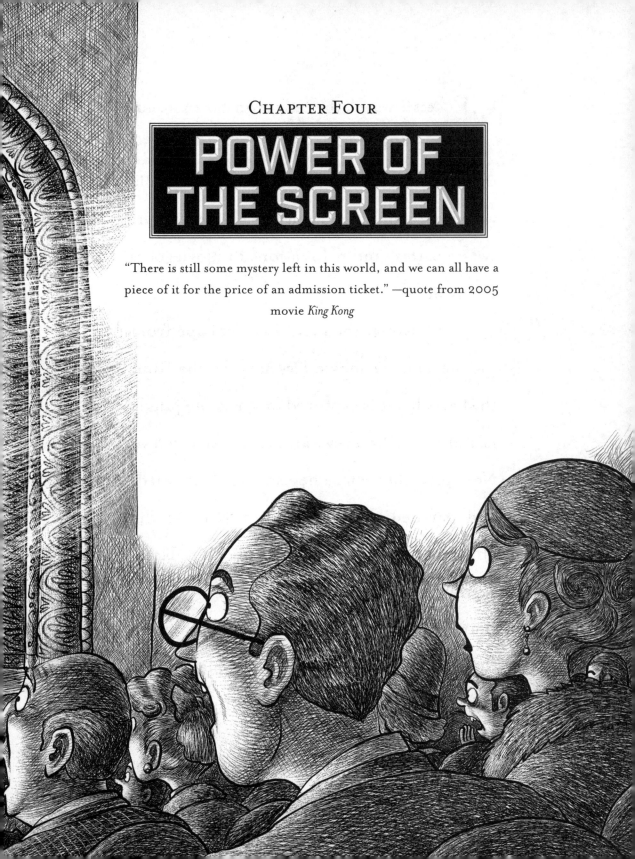

CHAPTER FOUR

POWER OF THE SCREEN

"There is still some mystery left in this world, and we can all have a piece of it for the price of an admission ticket." —quote from 2005 movie *King Kong*

Nessie wasn't the only monster to stomp frightfully through people's minds in the 1930s. At the same time, a colossal gorilla was also storming pop culture—inducing fear, sweaty palms, and palpitations in moviegoers everywhere.

It was Kong, the giant fictional ape from the blockbuster movie *King Kong*. In the film, the hairy beast is captured on a remote jungle island by a film crew, and then relocated to New York City where he's shackled, chained, and paraded in front of audiences as the "Eighth Wonder of the World." But Kong eventually breaks free, wreaking havoc as he thunders down city streets and shimmies up the Empire State Building. Ultimately, the hairy brute falls to his death while trying to protect the movie's heroine.

TREMBLING IN THEIR SEATS

So realistic were the film's special effects for that time—as comical as they may seem to us now—that moviegoers literally screamed out loud. Of course now we would laugh out loud. Consider the scene in which Kong is supposed to be gripping a male victim. In truth, a hairy fake ape is clutching what appears to be a plastic Ken doll!

Regardless, audiences were stunned as they exited the horror film. They poured out of theaters, observers noted, pale in the face and breathing heavily. As one cryptid researcher Dick Raynor remarked, in that moment, the "entire Western world was gripped by monster fever."

Researchers say that the Loch Ness connection here is undeniable. Especially when you consider the timing. *King Kong* debuted before sold-out New York and London theaters in the spring of 1933—just a few months before George Spicer thought he saw a plesiosaur-like beast rise up from Scotland's Loch Ness!

Could the fascination with a fictional beast inspire belief in another? Some researchers strongly believe so.

And there's an even more compelling corollary. The movie *King Kong* not only features an oversize ape, but also a long-necked water beast that fits George Spicer's exact description of Nessie! And the Nessie look-alike in the film is quite terrifying. In one scene it seizes a raft full of men in a lagoon, savagely killing them in its apparent thirst for blood.

CONSUMING THE MONSTER

Another thing about Nessie that proved irresistible starting in the 1930s—and continuing today—is the beast's capacity to make big bucks.

The long-necked glider has inspired a range of consumer goods, including even a Kellogg's cereal commerical! Yes, in a 1980's commercial, men in stylish kilts are seen peddling the breakfast flakes, just as their boat is lifted out of the water by a suddenly roused lake monster!

In the 1930s, Selfridges department store in London sold "Sandy," a plush, huggable Loch Ness Monster toy. There was also "Archibald," a wooden puzzle that appeared at around the same time (maybe Nessie's stuffier, tweed-wearing cousin?!).

In addition to the countless figurines and other kitschy souvenirs, Nessie and its likeness have been used to sell comics, movies, mustard, even floor polish.

Today, Scotland's Loch Ness draws about one million tourists, padding the local economy with about forty million extra dollars each year. Not too shabby, Nessie! But this money-making potential has to be carefully considered as we continue to explore the Loch Ness case.

DINO MANIA

This brings us to another important cultural factor in the fascination with a supposed Loch Ness creature. In the early decades of the 1900s, the world was preoccupied with all things prehistoric.

Many of America's most thrilling dinosaur bone discoveries were made in the 1870s through the early 1900s. It was during this period, nicknamed

the Great Dinosaur Rush, that explorers dug up bones belonging to such well-known stompers as *Stegosaurus* and *Allosaurus* in places like modern-day Montana and Wyoming. In museums around the world, crowds gaped at models of these giants, creatures larger than anything they'd ever seen.

And because life inspires art, and vice versa, dino mania spilled over into pop culture. Books and movies featured explorers making wild discoveries in far-off lands. Some of that was actually happening, as explorers at the time were also uncovering such marvels as Egypt's Valley of the Kings and the Mayan pyramids.

The idea of a "lost world," freshly discovered by modern-day humans, seemed tantalizing. But the concept was taken to the extreme. Consider Arthur Conan Doyle's 1912 hit, *The Lost World*, in which dinosaurs still roam freely across the Amazon unbeknownst to man. This fantasy/discovery genre is powerful even today, evidenced in video game series like Tomb Raider and Uncharted and in movie series such as Indiana Jones and Night at the Museum.

As we continue our investigation into cryptids, we must consider the power of cultural creations like *King Kong*. Such suggestive images stick to and invade our minds and can subtly bend our sense of reality.

BEAST WITH A BEAT

Nessie has even inspired a long list of pop songs and music. The diving lake monster seems to not play favorites either, having been featured in genres ranging from foxtrot and folk music to heavy metal and reggae! Some song titles include:

"Sea Serpent Polka" (1850)

"Boo, Boo. Here Comes the Loch Ness Monster" (1934)

"What a Whopper" (1961)

"Water Beastie" (1978)

"You'll Never Find a Nessie in the Zoo" (1983)

Even pop music icon Sting, when still with his former band the Police, references the beast—a metaphor for something dark and foreboding—in these lyrics from the 1983 song "Synchronicity II."

Many miles away
Something crawls from the slime
At the bottom of a dark Scottish lake. . . .

SEARCH WITH CARE!

Eighty years of searching for Nessie, using scuba divers, boats, submarines, and dredging equipment, has created its own kind of monster in Loch Ness. This stunning deep cleft of a lake, one of Scotland's greatest treasures, is starting to fill up with junk.

The decade's worth of people (and their equipment) who have scoured the lake in hopes of finding some alleged dinosaur-like animal have left a filthy trail. Among this debris are even plastic monster pieces abandoned after earlier failed hoaxes! (In 2016, a fake monster that was spied in the lake with a robot turned out to be a prop from a movie shot in 1969!)

Another concern? The fleets of boats and other equipment used to plumb the lake accidentally bring unwanted guests with them, including the American flatworm. Such invasive species, which hitch rides from elsewhere, wreak havoc on native plant and animal communities.

CHAPTER FIVE

SCIENCE: THE ULTIMATE SLEUTH

"When you have eliminated the impossible, whatever remains, however improbable, must be the truth." —Sherlock Holmes, a fictional character created by British author Sir Arthur Conan Doyle

So, how do we cut through the fog surrounding Loch Ness and make a clear conclusion about the potential for a real-life Nessie?

We've discussed how pop culture, greed, and the temptation to trick and deceive can influence public opinion. Is there an unbiased way to evaluate the likelihood that a lake monster truly exists?

Of course there is—that great truth seeker is science! Its methods and the tools and technologies it relies on provide ways to parse fact from fiction and get to the bottom of whatever may—or may not—be lurking at the bottom of the seven-hundred-fifty-foot-deep Loch Ness.

Science is like the strictest, tough-as-nails teacher you've ever had. It's demanding and rigorous. But it's also comforting. The equation 1 + 1 = 2 will never change. Neither will the value of pi (π = 3.14).

If our hypothesis is that a plesiosaur-like beast inhabits Scotland's Loch Ness, then we have a major burden of proof to overcome. It's like in a courtroom. Only instead of a prosecutor making a case, it's the monster believer who has to prove that Nessie exists. He or she has a jury, too, but in science this group consists of the best and brightest

EXHIBIT "A"

scientists in a particular field (This is called "peer review"). These experts must then be convinced, beyond a reasonable doubt, that what the monster believer is pitching to them is true.

Just like in big criminal cases, the most compelling evidence in science is cold, hard, irrefutable proof, such as DNA, physical specimens, blood samples, or bones! Unfortunately for Nessie lovers, this kind of evidence just hasn't been found.

EXHIBIT "B"

CAUGHT ON CAMERA?

So, in the case of Nessie, what kinds of evidence would you hope to find? Bones and fossils. Ideally, a whole carcass (yuck!), or the living creature itself. However, none of these things have been discovered as proof of the lake monster's existence.

But that hasn't kept the hunters and researchers from trying to capture evidence, especially on camera.

Pictures have been snapped, and some tantalizing film sequences have been taken, too. The mysterious black-and-white footage captured on film by engineer Tim Dinsdale in 1960 is the most well-known and studied. In this fuzzy recording, a suspicious object appears to be wading across Loch Ness. And when it was later scrutinized by photographic experts with the Royal Air Force in 1966, they acknowledged it could be "an unknown animate object."

Today's experts, including longtime Loch Ness researcher Adrian Shine, are mostly convinced that the object captured on Dinsdale's famous mini-film is a boat.

Many other lenses have also been aimed at the famous loch. Remember F. W. Holiday from the beginning of our story? He visited Loch Ness repeatedly in the 1960s along with the Loch Ness Phenomena Investigation Bureau. From dawn to dusk, team members took turns manning large high-powered telescopic lenses pointed toward the lake. After seasons of such marathon watches, though, nothing exceptional was ever discovered.

Underwater photography has been tried too, but it's a challenge due to the murky nature of the loch's waters. Peat particles, pieces of partly decomposed mosses and other plants, are suspended in the lake like bits of tea leaves floating in a mug.

But that challenge didn't deter researcher, patent-holder, and lawyer Robert H. Rines. In the 1970s, this graduate of the Massachusetts Institute of Technology captured some of the most convincing images of a possible Loch Ness beast. In one, Rines was convinced he saw the beast's flipper.

This grainy underwater shot—complicated by the floating peat particles—did not pass muster with the scientific community. Yet Rines remained generally convinced of what he saw, once remarking: "They can just call me crazy, and that's okay by me."

Clever and undaunted, the man who as a young boy once played violin with Albert Einstein sought other ingenious methods.

He tried attracting Nessie using pheromones, the animal world's equivalent of perfume. And to improve his chances of snagging quality underwater shots, he also explored using dolphins to carry the cameras!

BEWARE THE "EXPERT"

Today, the word "expert" is tossed around all the time. We hear it referenced across media: on television, in newspapers, and in a lot of advertising. The truth is that becoming an expert on a subject is serious business. While passion and interest are great, just because someone has written a book, created a website, or started an organization about a topic does not qualify them as an expert.

Expertise requires intensive study on a specific topic through a respected institution. Even a PhD or MD can be suspect. For instance, a doctorate in philosophy or psychology is impressive, but when it comes to the study of cryptids, one should rely on specialists in fields such as zoology, ecology, paleontology, or systematics (the study of how the earth's diverse life-forms are classified and organized).

SUPERSONIC

Rines went on to assist with other scouting technology, namely sonar. This approach, which uses the power of sound waves to locate objects, seemed to Nessie hunters like a surefire way to pinpoint the beast.

For over forty years, a variety of sonar projects have been coordinated on Loch Ness. Many of these have been large-scale systematic or dragnet-style searches. One single effort in 1982, for instance, logged fifteen hundred hours of patrol time!

The most exhaustive sonar survey, though, was known as "Operation Deepscan," conducted in 1987 by Loch Ness expert Adrian Shine. During this expensive and intensive search, a fleet of no fewer than twenty-four boats was used to scour Loch Ness. Side-by-side, these boats formed a "sonar curtain" that swept the entire loch.

While nothing stood out as remarkable, there remains, to this day, three inexplicable "hits" made by the sonar equipment. These "wobbly scratches," as they've been described, cannot be fully explained.

DREDGED LOCHS

There has been no shortage of ideas when it comes to pinpointing the Loch Ness Monster. The bottom of the lake has been scraped, or dredged. Wide nets have been cast out. Submarines, including a yellow one named *Viperfish*, have been enlisted to plumb the depths of Loch Ness. And you've heard of SUVs, but what about AUVs? Autonomous Underwater Vehicles, which are basically underwater robots, have also been let loose inside the loch!

Yet, despite all of the inventive, tech-savvy methods tried, not a single beastie bone, fossil, or other form of solid evidence has ever turned up.

NO HOME FOR SUCH A BEAST

There are other biological considerations to make about the likelihood of a looming beast in Loch Ness.

Loch Ness is quite large—but this is still insufficient to support an alleged thirty-foot-long creature requiring hefty amounts of food to survive.

The leftover dinosaur hypothesis is also impossible, geologically speaking. If Nessie is some descendent of the plesiosaurs, how could her ancestors have survived the Ice Age of the more recent Pleistocene epoch, which was about 2.5 million to 11,700 years ago?

In fact, all of Scotland lay crushed under a half-mile-thick sheet of ice just as recently as eighteen thousand years ago! To exist, Nessie or her ancestors would have to have been frozen, then come back to life: an earthly impossibility!

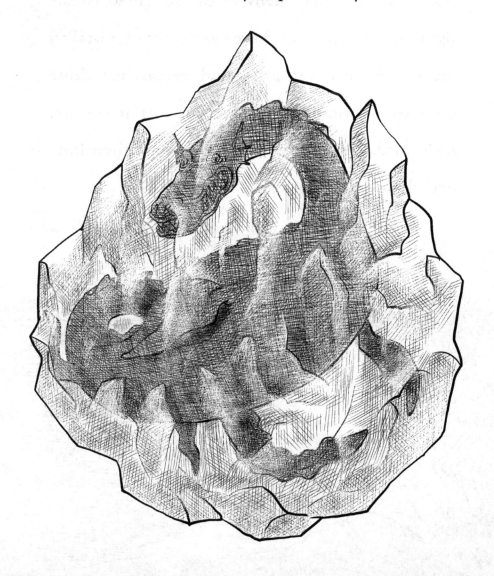

SEEING THINGS

It's most likely that many of the so-called Nessie sightings over the years have been cases of mistaken identity. As silly as it may sound, researchers think the most commonly confused culprits are otters, seals, birds (especially cormorants, with their long necks), and floating logs.

Take for instance the incident in which a journalist by the name of Alex Campbell was convinced that he'd seen a creature in Loch Ness. It was thirty feet long, he later told a reporter, craning its head above water to look around. Days later, however, the man retracted his story. What he thought was a long-necked lake beast turned out to be little more than a flock of cormorants! Apparently Campbell had reconsidered his excited testimony and realized his error. His defense: Several of the birds had formed a line in the water and appeared "in the poor light and at first glance just like the body or humps of the Monster."

There may be other tricky phenomenon at play too, including large mats of vegetation, which have been known to bubble up or inflate; or unusual waves in the water called seiches. Seiches at Loch Ness are formed by strong prevailing winds that push water in one direction. Then, to backfill the displaced water, those waves start rocking in the opposite direction. These crazy waves may rock on for several days until they release all the wind energy locked up in them!

MUSHY MEMORIES

So how can humans make such colossal mistakes? Confusing a log, for instance, with a large slimy lake monster?! Well, for one, we're not perfect—especially if we're tired, emotional, or stressed out.

Secondly, most of us simply do not understand how memory works. We tend to think our experiences at the time they are happening are instantly and precisely uploaded to our brains. And then later we can simply download these pure and perfect little "bytes" anytime we'd like. Not so. In reality, the act of remembering is an act of building and recreating. In fact, one memory expert describes this recollection process as more like "putting puzzle pieces together than retrieving a video recording."

Even if our brains are able to capture an event relatively accurately, these images and details over time can still become distorted. For instance, many people will form memories of things that never happened.

So what does this mean for those hundreds, even thousands, of eyewitness accounts of a Loch Ness beast? Even when they come from the most passionate voices, these accounts must be considered carefully—and can *never* serve as hard evidence.

As you can see, in the end, science—with all its methods, tools, and technologies—is the only way to truly track down a monster. In the case of Nessie, science's bright light has lit up many of the loch's deep dark secrets. While there may not be a leftover dinosaur hibernating in its depths, there are still many other unknown marvels!

DEFLATED? DESPAIRING? NOT SO FAST

"The great tragedy of Science—the slaying of a beautiful hypothesis by an ugly fact." —Thomas Henry Huxley, an English biologist

So there's probably not a surviving plesiosaur or other blubbery beast paddling in Scotland's Loch Ness. It's a bit disappointing. However, it doesn't mean that there aren't other discoveries to be made there.

For instance, local expert Adrian Shine wonders if some of the cases of mistaken identity might trace back to sturgeon—large fish (some measure up to twelve feet!) that may be sneaking into the loch from the Atlantic Ocean to hunt for new breeding grounds. A new fish species would be exciting to document, in addition to the salmon, pike, char, and stickleback fish that already course through the lake's chilly waters!

As far as Nessie goes, science may seem a spoilsport. But try not to hold a grudge for too long. As paleontologist and cryptid skeptic Donald R. Prothero once said, "Scientists are not inherently negative sourpusses who want to rain on everyone else's parade."

Serious researchers are simply striving to get to the bottom of questions, oftentimes critical ones relating to medicine, our world's supplies of clean air and water, alternative energy sources, national security, and more.

And beyond the green emerald hills of Scotland, there remains so much more on planet Earth to investigate and explore—especially in our oceans and other deep waters. According to the U.S. National Oceanic and Atmospheric Administration, for instance, a whopping ninety-five percent of our oceans still need to be explored!

Not to mention there are other creepy cryptids out there to scout, study, and scrutinize—like the others being investigated in this monster series, such as Bigfoot and other monsters feared throughout history, such as werewolves and zombies!

As long as there are more mysteries to unravel and bizarre wonders to explore, then the spirit of Nessie must surely live on.

Main Sources

Campbell, John Gregorson. *Superstitions of the Highlands and Islands of Scotland*. Glasgow: James MacLehose and Sons, 1900.

Darnton, John. "Loch Ness: Fiction Is Stranger Than Truth," *The New York Times*, March 20, 1994.

Holiday, F. W. *The Great Orm of Loch Ness*. New York: W. W. Norton & Company, 1969.

Loxton, Daniel and Donald R. Prothero. *Abominable Science! Origins of the Yeti, Nessie, and Other Famous Cryptids*. New York: Columbia University Press, 2013.

Martin, Douglas. "Robert Rines, Inventor and Monster Hunter, Dies at 87," *The New York Times*, November 7, 2009.

Williams, Gareth. *A Monstrous Commotion: The Mysteries of Loch Ness*. United Kingdom: Orion Publishing, 2015.

FOR FURTHER READING

The Internet runneth over with Loch Ness Monster information, much of which is bogus. (If you were to believe the World Wide Web, then there's some kind of breaking news about Nessie almost *every* day!)

If you do search online, focus on articles written by scientific authorities or by reputable science media sources like *Scientific American, New Scientist,* and *National Geographic.*

A great website to search is the Loch Ness and Morar Project website at lochnessproject.org. This is the organization led by naturalist and local expert Adrian Shine, who's been researching Loch Ness for more than forty years.